Tara the starfish likes to do lots of sport.
Lee the lobster is Tara's coach.

Tara and Lee are at the Splash Pool Sports Club. They like to train there.

Tara lifts some big snail shells to keep fit.

Tara trains hard. She likes to run in the woods in the morning ...

... and she likes to swim in the pool at night.
But training can be hard!

One night, Lee is waiting to check
Tara's speeds.

Tara is not at the pool, so Lee
steps out to look for her.

"What is Tara up to?" thinks Lee.
He sets off to the sports track.

When he gets there, Lee flicks on his
torch and spots Tara. She is not training.

Tara is in her car. "I do so much sport, I am worn out!" she groans. "I need a little rest!"

Spelling and writing

Cover the words below. Say the first word (*step*). Ask the child to repeat the word and tap out the phonemes in order with his or her fingers, saying each phoneme (*s-t-e-p*) and then writing the graphemes to spell the word. Repeat this with the other words.

step   rest

train   splash

Understanding the story   Ask the questions below to make sure that the children understand the story.

1 What does Tara like to do? (page 1)

2 Where does Tara go? (page 10)

Assessment

Say the phonemes

Point to each grapheme in turn and ask the child to say the corresponding phoneme. Note whether the child is correct each time and go back to any incorrect ones.

Next, cover the graphemes. Say a phoneme and ask the child to write the corresponding graphemes. Prompt the child to write /ur/ in two different ways. Practise any that are incorrect.

ar	ure	ow	air
er	ur	ear	oi

Read the words

Ask the child to sound out a word and then blend the phonemes and say the word. Repeat this with the other words.

sport   crunch   groans

script   crisps